Healthy Hearty Helpings

Anne Dinshah

Quick aɴd easy,
delicious recipes for
the hearty eater, athlete,
for vegan survival at college, or
for others who really don't
like to cook but love to
eat healthful food

The American Vegan Society
56 Dinshah Lane - P.O. Box H
Malaga, New Jersey 08328

This cookbook is bound using the Otabind Easy-Open process, to lie flat for easier use. This combines improved bookbinding technology with a special free-floating cover, to produce an unusually durable, high-quality, user-friendly book. Open the book at any page, run a finger firmly down the inside spine (if necessary, at first) and the page will stay open where desired.

I thank my parents for the way they raised me, and for their life work on behalf of the animals and fellow humans; special appreciation to Mom (Freya Dinshah) for encouraging me in the kitchen from an early age; to Dad (H. Jay Dinshah) for the typography, illustrations and design of this book; and my husband (Curt Hamre) and many of our friends, for their taste-trials and helpful suggestions.

Anne Dinshah

The American Vegan Society expresses its gratitude
for the kindness of the following members whose generosity
has helped to make this printing possible:

Ted D. Barnett, M.D. and Carol Hee Barnett
Mrs. William A. Cave
Norman L. Conaway
Joanne Goleman
Linda Kwallek
Victoria Moran
Dr. Jules Oaklander
David Opperman
Stephanie Schuler
Jay and Jackie Steinberg
Dawn R. Vinson
A Friend

1st Edition: June, 1999
ISBN 0-942401-19-0

Contents

Illustrations:

✿ *Also seen in front-cover color collage, numbered clockwise from top left.*

Introduction

Over a ten year span I lived in a total of six states while studying, rowing, and/or coaching at five different universities. During that time I made some observations about young adults in general. They have no time, like to eat, have little access to kitchen appliances, and most don't eat enough fruits and vegetables.

I've always taken the cooking skill for granted. Look in the fridge, throw something together, and then wish I had measured things so there could be a recipe when my friends asked for it. Through recent years of educating collegiate athletes about basic nutrition, I realized the need for simple recipes that taste good. There is also a growing general interest in vegan/vegetarian cooking. People want to learn, but only if it is easy to do.

Most of these recipes were created when I only had access to a small refrigerator, one-burner hot plate, microwave oven and toaster oven, and a blender (my favorite kitchen appliance). The measuring utensils used were not particularly accurate. The beauty of this is that these recipes are easy to make and hard to mess up. When you just throw it together, skip a step, or mis-measure a bit, sometimes it tastes even better! However, please try to do them as written first.

Lately Americans have become more concerned about fat and calories. I believe it is helpful to know how to calculate these things to assist in making major changes in food habits, such as when a person is unhealthy, at an undesirable weight, or has a poor energy level. Get professional guidance if needed.

However, good health, well-being and top performance are more than just calories, and are often described as a combination of diet, exercise, and other factors. Let's not use that four-letter word *diet*; let's just have good nutrition instead. Stock your kitchen with vegetables, fruits, whole-grains (including breads and cereals), legumes (peas, beans, lentils), nuts and seeds. These are the vegan staples.

Although I have taught basic nutrition to athletes, it is better for you to learn directly from those who taught me. Recommended literature includes *Vegan Nutrition: Pure And Simple*, Michael Klaper, M.D.; *A Basic Course In Vegetarian And Vegan Nutrition*, George Eisman, R.D.; *Nutrition For Vegetarians*, A. & C. Thrash, M.D.s; *Becoming Vegetarian*, Melina, Davis, Harrison, R.D.s; and Dr. Harris' article in *VEGANISM: Getting Started*. It also helps if you have the opportunity to attend vegetarian or vegan conventions.

As far as the calorie-count goes on a regular basis, here's my way of thinking: First of all, who enjoys doing the math? Second, when one feels great, it's more fun to be doing something else. Third, since when have people eaten standard size servings? Therefore the serving sizes in this book refer to how much a healthy active young adult might eat. One or two servings is typical although an intense athlete may eat more.

Exercise is extremely important. Some of us may swim, run, bike, row, etc., five or six days a week. It is usually part of my job to exercise and stay one step ahead of the athletes I coach. However, the important thing is to just get up and do something, even if it simply starts out as a half-hour walk twice a week. You'll begin to feel better and can gradually increase your exercise.

Breakfast. If it's too early for cooking, then don't; but eat well. Maybe it's grab a bowl of cereal and fruit, or try something new from the Breakfast Items section or the Desserts section. The desserts are so healthful they're not just for dessert any more. One can make a big batch of muffins, cobbler, or cake on Sunday so breakfast's ready for the week.

Lunch is important, but dinner is when I have more time to cook interesting things and invite friends to join me. That's probably why there seem to be so many main dishes and desserts in this book. They are the tastiest ways to impress friends.

Note: Different ovens vary widely in accuracy. Toaster ovens may run cooler (requiring a higher setting or longer cooking time) than range ovens. Toaster ovens also tend to brown the top of the food sooner. If browning too soon, cover with aluminum foil. It helps to know how to test if the item is "done." For example: with apples or potatoes: stab with fork to test. Cakes, muffins: insert toothpick in center and it should come out dry, not sticky. With experience you can often tell by the aroma.

I hope you have as much fun with these recipes as I do. One suggestion is to give three of these recipes to three of your friends. Have them make these dishes on the same night and bring them to your house so you can all eat together. Another idea is to go to a friend's house one evening and have the friend come to your home the next week. Continue this until you have tried all the recipes. Your social life will improve as more friends want to get in on the fun. (You can even buy two or more copies of this cookbook!)

Best of luck and happy eating!

Unfamiliar Ingredients

One of my goals in writing this book is to make it easy to cook good vegan food. I do most of my shopping in a grocery store, though I may not find everything I want there. Sometimes I go to a good health food store.

A few recipes contain ingredients with which some of you may be unfamiliar. I tried to include them all here; but I well remember the athlete I coached who had never even tried a grapefruit (a pomegranate, I could understand).

Afghan bread: a large rectangular flat bread, approx. 9x24"; great for pizza crust

Basil: an herb that can be used fresh or dried, amount dependent on personal taste. 1 tsp. dry = approx. 5 leaves

Cane juice, granulated: like brown sugar, but unrefined, naturally processed

Caraway seeds: found on spice shelf

Carob powder: ground toasted carob pods with chocolatey flavor; can be used instead of cocoa powder.

Cashew nuts: use raw, unsalted

Cilantro: a fresh herb that looks similar to parsley, but has a stronger flavor; often used in Mexican dishes

Coriander: dried cilantro

Cumin: a spice that adds a gentle warm (not hot/spicy) flavor

Currants: like tiny raisins

Dill: an herb, fresh or dried

Kale: a green leafy vegetable

Kelp granules: powdered seaweed; can substitute for salt

Leeks: long green mild onion

Maple syrup: liquid sweetener from maple tree sap

Nutritional yeast: a food yeast, fortified

Pita: a middle-eastern flat bread with a pocket that can be filled with foods

Portabella mushrooms: have a "meaty" flavor, and come in a variety of sizes

Pumpkin pie spices: a mix of cinnamon, nutmeg, allspice, and ginger.

Rice syrup: a thick liquid sweetener

Sausage, vegan/meatless: usually a ready to cook or eat mixture of textured vegetable protein and spices

Soya powder: made from cooked soy beans

Spearmint: a garden mint/herb

Stuffable mushrooms: like big button mushrooms

Tahini: sesame seed butter

Tamari: soy sauce

Tapioca granules: a thickening, jelling agent

Tempeh: a fermented soy bean product

Vegan soy mayonnaise: now available ready-made

Wheat germ: found in the cereal aisle

Breakfast
Items

Peach-Oatmeal Breakfast Muffins

Bananamania

2 bananas
1 Tbs. tahini
¼ cup raisins

Optional:
2 Tbs. wheat germ
1 Tbs. shredded coconut
1 tsp. carob powder

Mash bananas. Mix in other ingredients. Eat.
For a hearty breakfast, serve on whole wheat toast or crisp rice cakes.

Berry Jumble
Makes 6 servings

2 cups blueberries
1 apple
10 dates
½ tsp. cinnamon
2 Tbs. oil
¼ cup water
1 cup granulated cane juice,
  or brown sugar
1 cup whole wheat pastry flour
1 Tbs. wheat germ

Wash blueberries. Wash and chop apple. Pit and chop dates.

Mix berries, apple, dates, and cinnamon.

Mix oil, water, sugar, and flour.

Partly combine the two mixtures in a jumbled manner.

Put in a loaf pan and pat the top down lightly. Sprinkle wheat germ on top. Bake at 350° F. for 45 minutes. Serve warm or cold.

Great with soy milk or soy ice cream.

Cranberry Sauce
Makes 5 to 6 cups

1 lb. cranberries
2 cups raisins
2 apples
3 cups water
2 tsp. cinnamon
1 cup maple syrup

Wash cranberries. Wash, core and chop apples. Place all ingredients except maple syrup into a medium size pot.

Bring to boil. Remove from heat, and let stand for 10 minutes.

Stir in the maple syrup. Chill and serve. Can be used as a spread on bread, or on hot cereal.

Fruit Castles
Makes 8 servings

1 cup orange juice
2 cups apple juice
¾ cup tapioca granules
1 cup maple syrup
1 cup raisins
2 apples
2 tsp. pumpkin pie spices
   (cinnamon, nutmeg, allspice, ginger)
20 oz. can crushed pineapple
   (2½ cups pineapple and juice)
1 cup seedless grapes
2 cups soy milk
4 Tbs. wheat germ

On medium heat, bring to a boil the orange juice, apple juice, juice from pineapple, tapioca, maple syrup and raisins. Stir frequently to prevent sticking. Reduce heat; continue stirring. Cook until the juice thickens and raisins swell.

Wash and chop apples and grapes; mix into hot juice. Mix in spices and pineapple. Cool in fridge.

Serve in individual bowls. The fruit makes a castle with soy milk as a moat. Sprinkle wheat germ on top of fruit.

Kiwi Caress

Makes 1½ cups or 2 servings

3 kiwi fruits
½ lb. tofu (firm)
2 Tbs. orange juice
4 Tbs. maple syrup
Dash of ginger

Wash, peel, and chop kiwis into a bowl. Blenderize remaining ingredients, and pour over kiwis. Serve.

You may also like to decorate by saving a slice of kiwi and placing it on top.

Kiwi Pie
12 servings

6 kiwi fruit
2 cups dates
3 apples
3 cups water
2 tsp. cinnamon
3 cups granola, puffed wheat,
  corn flakes, or other cereal

Wash and chop apples. Peel and chop kiwis. Pit and chop dates.

Place all ingredients except cereal in a pot, and bring to a boil. Remove from heat, and stir briefly.

Put cereal in casserole dish, and pour the kiwi mixture over it.

Chill overnight. Serve with non-dairy yogurt, soy milk, or vegan "ice cream."

Peach-Oatmeal
Breakfast Muffins
Makes 12 large muffins

Wet ingredients:
  ¾ cup applesauce
  1 cup raspberry (or other fruit) juice
  3 bananas
  ½ cup maple syrup
  3 peaches
  1 cup strawberries (optional)

Dry ingredients:
  1 tsp. baking soda
  1 Tbs. corn starch
  3 cups whole wheat pastry flour
    (or unbleached flour)
  1 cup oats
  1 tsp. cinnamon
  ½ tsp. ground cloves
  ¾ cup dates
  ½ cup walnuts

Wash and chop peaches and strawberries Mash bananas. Chop dates and walnuts. Mix all wet ingredients. Mix all dry ingredients. Pour one mixture into the other, and stir. Place in non-stick muffin tins. Bake at 375° F. for 30 minutes or until done.

Stuffed Apples
Makes 3

3 apples
¼ cup dried apricots
¼ cup shelled walnuts
¼ cup white grape juice concentrate
1 Tbs. wheat germ
½ tsp. cinnamon

Finely chop apricots and walnuts; mix them with the next 3 ingredients. Let stand 10 minutes to begin to absorb the juice.

Meanwhile, wash the apples. Keep the apples whole, except slice off the top of each and save it.

Core the apples. Put apricot/walnut stuffing in apples, overfilling them. Replace apple tops.

Gently prick each apple on its sides with a knife point (to avoid bursting during baking).

Bake at 375° F. for 30 minutes or until done. Serve with your favorite vegan (nut-, seed-, soy-, or rice-) cream.

Appetizers and Dips

Hummus

Black Bean Hummus
Makes 2½ cups

1½ cups black beans (canned or cooked)
1½ Tbs. tahini
1 tsp. olive oil
2 Tbs. lemon juice
2 Tbs. water
10 big leaves of fresh basil
1 tsp. cumin
Dash of cayenne pepper

Blenderize all ingredients. Serve as a dip for pita or crackers.

Cucumber Hors d'oeuvres
Makes 24 bite-sized hors d'oeuvres

6 slices pumpernickel bread
½ cup Sesame Sandwich Spread
   (see recipe)
2 small cucumbers,
   pickling kind preferred
a few sprigs of parsley or dill, fresh

Cut bread into quarters (squares or triangles). Spread the spread on the bread.

Wash and slice cucumbers; put a cucumber slice on each piece of bread.

Garnish with parsley or dill. Serve.

Dill Me Dip
Makes ¾ cup

½ cup soy mayonnaise
¼ cup water
dill, dry or fresh chopped

Mix all ingredients. Serve with crackers or stick-salad items (carrot, celery), cauliflower pieces, etc.

Hummus

2 cups cooked garbanzos
    (chick peas, 16 oz. can)
2 Tbs. tahini
2 Tbs. lemon juice
4 Tbs. water (approx.)
    fresh, or drained from garbanzos
½ tsp. celery salt
½ tsp. cumin
1 tsp. diced cilantro or parsley
5 cherry tomatoes

Drain garbanzos; put in blender with tahini, lemon juice, and enough water (or their liquid) to blend. Pour into bowl.

Wash and chop the tomatoes into halves or quarters. Mix into bowl with all remaining ingredients. Serve chilled with toasted pita bread, tortilla chips, or crackers.

I Love Dip
Makes 2 cups

1 16-oz. can vegetarian refried beans
1/8 cup water
20 pitted black olives

Mix beans and water. Chop olives and mix in. Serve as dip for crackers, celery, carrots, broccoli flowerettes, etc.

Fresh Veggie Stew, with whole-wheat bread

Soups and Stews

Broccoli Soup
Makes 4 servings

1 large head broccoli
1 large potato
1 celery stalk
1½ cups water
10 fresh basil leaves
1 Tbs. tamari soy sauce

Wash, chop, and cook the vegetables in water.
Blenderize all ingredients.
Reheat while stirring.

Celery Soup
Makes 4 to 6 servings

4 celery stalks
2 carrots
3 potatoes
¼ head cabbage
2 to 6 cups water
1 tsp. cumin
¼ cup cilantro, fresh
½ tsp. celery salt
Dash of red pepper

Wash, chop, and cook vegetables in 2 cups of water. Blenderize all ingredients (half at a time, in a typical blender). Add sufficient additional water to achieve desired consistency.

Variation: When putting through the blender, put most of the chopped carrots in one blenderful, and most of the celery in the other batch. The two batches should be gently swirled (not mixed) as they are poured into soup bowls for serving.

Fresh Veggie Stew
Makes 3 servings

1 cup fresh (or frozen) lima beans
1 cup fresh (or frozen) green beans
1 potato
1 carrot
1 zucchini squash
2 large tomatoes
3 cups water

Wash and chop vegetables. Place all ingredients in stew pot. Bring to boil, reduce heat and continue cooking until potato is tender.

Lentil Stew
Makes 8-10 servings

1 cup lentils
4 cups water
4 potatoes
½ head broccoli
¼ head cabbage
1 onion
3 celery stalks
3 carrots
10 mushrooms
4 tomatoes
**2 cups vegetable juice or tomato juice
(canned or bottled)**

Wash lentils. Place in large stewpot with water. Wash and chop all vegetables; put into pot.

Bring to boil, then simmer about 45 minutes or until lentils and potatoes are tender. Stir the juice into the stew.

Serve with air-popped popcorn (no butter), crackers, or warm taco shells.

Invite friends over to share this; or you can freeze leftover stew for later use

Mushroom Soup
Makes 6 cups

4 medium potatoes
2 cups water
1 celery stalk
1 lb. mushrooms
½ cup soy milk
1 Tbs. soy sauce (tamari)
¼ tsp. red pepper (optional)

Wash and chop potatoes, celery, and mushrooms. Cook in water until potatoes are tender.

Remove and reserve some of the mushrooms; blenderize the rest of the soup (with the remaining ingredients); half at a time will fit in the blender.

Return soup to pot. Mix in reserved mushrooms.

Optional: reserve 3 cups of soup; refrigerate and use in making Green Bean Casserole (see recipe) next day.

Potato Leek Soup
Makes 5 cups

4 potatoes
1 large leek
1 celery stalk
2 cups water

Wash and chop the vegetables; cook them in the water until tender.

Blenderize (can leave some veggies unblended for chunky style, or blenderize all for creamy).

Happy Salad, Curt's Cucumber Salad....
with whole-wheat crackers, Triple-Topped Potatoes

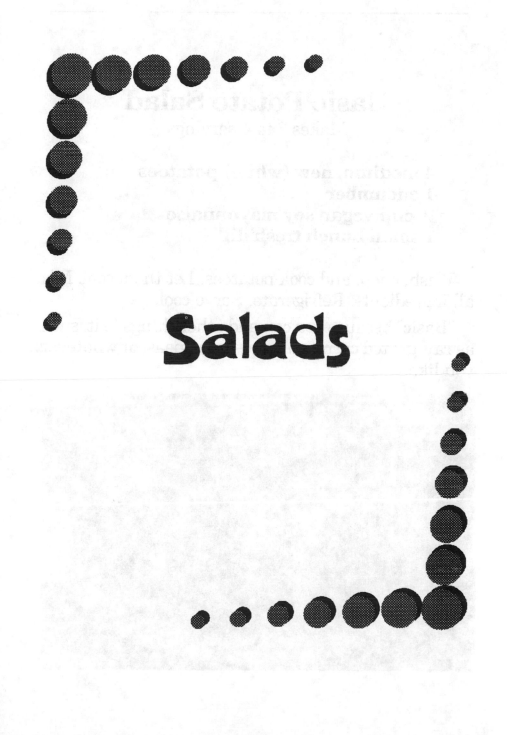

Salads

Basic Potato Salad
Makes 3 to 4 servings

4 medium, new (white) potatoes
1 cucumber
½ cup vegan soy mayonnaise
1 small bunch fresh dill

Wash, chop, and cook potatoes. Let them cool. Mix all ingredients. Refrigerate. Serve cool.

"Basic" because you can add other things to it, such as raw grated carrot, or a few green peas, or whatever you like.

Curt's Cucumber Salad
Makes 2 servings

2 cucumbers (pickling kind)
3 plum tomatoes
small handful fresh cilantro (optional)
¼ green bell pepper
¼ tsp. salt
2 tsp. lemon juice
2 tsp. olive oil

Wash and finely chop cucumbers, tomatoes, pepper, and cilantro. Mix all ingredients.
Serve with baked tortilla chips.

Easy Beany Salad
Makes 6 servings

1 small head red leaf lettuce
2 cups black beans (canned, drained)
1 tomato

Wash lettuce and rip into pieces. Place in large bowl. Wash and chop tomato. Add beans, and mix everything together.

Serve with Tomato Basil Dressing (see recipe).

Fireburst Salad
Serves 2

2 carrots
¼ head cabbage
½ cup raisins
½ cup water
3 heaping Tbs. soy mayonnaise
5 leaves green leaf lettuce

Put raisins and water in microwave bowl covered with plate. Microwave on high for 2 to 3 minutes, until the raisins swell. Drain.

Wash and grate carrots and cabbage; combine these with the raisins and soy mayonnaise.

Arrange lettuce leaves in a star shape on plate. Place mixed ingredients in center.

Fruit Salad
Makes 4 servings

2 kiwis
2 bananas
1 grapefruit
1 orange
10 large strawberries
¼ cup orange juice

Peel all fruits except strawberries. Wash strawberries and trim off hulls. Cut up fruit. Pour orange juice on top to keep bananas from browning.

Mix. Serve with topping of non-dairy soy yogurt.

Happy Salad

1 ear fresh corn on the cob
½ cup green olives
2 celery stalks
1 can (about 2 cups) black beans
2 tsp. apple cider vinegar
2 tsp. olive oil

Husk the corn and cut from cob. Wash and chop celery. Mix all ingredients and serve.

Million Bean Salad

Feeds 10, great for potlucks and parties

2 cups lima beans, fresh or frozen
2 cups green beans, fresh or frozen
2 cups wax beans, fresh or frozen
2 cups black beans (canned)
2 cups great northern beans (canned)
2 cups pinto beans (canned)
2 cucumbers
water
4 big leaves fresh basil
10 leaves fresh spearmint
1 Tbs. olive oil
2 Tbs. lemon juice

Wash and chop green and wax beans. Put in pot with limas and enough water to cook beans (bring to boil then simmer on low).

Drain and combine all other beans in large bowl. Wash and finely chop cucumbers and herbs. Drain cooked beans. Combine all ingredients. Mix well. Chill and serve.

Rainbow Potato Salad
Makes 10 servings,
great for potlucks and parties

20 small red potatoes
2 cups water
1½ cups peas
1 small red bell pepper
1 small yellow bell pepper
1/8 head red cabbage
1 carrot

Dressing:
2 Tbs. flaxseed oil
1 Tbs. nutritional yeast
¼ tsp. kelp granules
1 tsp. lemon juice
1 tsp. soy sauce
1 tsp. caraway seeds

Scrub and chop potatoes in half; add the water and cook them. When potatoes are tender, remove from water and allow to cool.

Put peas in the water and reboil. Wash and chop peppers; mix them in and remove pot from heat. After one minute, drain. Meanwhile, wash and shred cabbage and carrots.

Mix all dressing ingredients. Combine all vegetables and mix in the dressing.

Simple Summer Salad
Serves 2

**5 large leaves of leaf lettuce,
 red or green
1 large tomato
½ cucumber
1 can white or black beans
 (drained, about 2 cups)
¼ cup raisins
1 small summer squash,
 zucchini or yellow**

Wash all vegetables. Chop tomato, cucumbers, and squash. Rip lettuce into pieces. Mix all ingredients. Eat as is or with your favorite dressing.

Dressings, Spreads, Gravies

Basic Mushroom Gravy
Makes 3 cups

20 whole button mushrooms
1½ cups vegetable broth
½ cup water
2 Tbs. corn starch
1 Tbs. soy sauce
Seasonings to taste (optional)

Wash and chop mushrooms. Stir corn starch into the water; then mix into the vegetable broth. Add mushrooms, soy sauce, and seasonings; mix again. Heat on high. Stir until it boils and begins to thicken. Remove from heat.

Allow to cool slightly and continue to thicken. Serve on Celery-Mushroom Stuffing (see recipe), Smashed Potatoes (see recipe), or other vegetable dish.

Hummus Sauce
Makes 2 cups

1½ cups garbanzos, (canned, drained)
¾ cup water,
   fresh or drained from garbanzos
1 Tbs. tahini
½ tsp. dried basil
1 Tbs. lemon juice
1 tsp. cumin
½ tsp. chili powder

Blenderize all ingredients. Serve over vegetables such as "Cheesy" Veggies (see recipe) for a delicious cheese alternative.

Olive Butter
Makes ½ cup

**1 cup green olives
(canned, pitted, and drained)
10 leaves fresh basil
10 leaves fresh mint**

Wash herbs. Blenderize all ingredients.

To serve, spread Olive Butter lightly on bagel, bread, or toast.

Note: Herbs may be varied.

Pesto For Pasta
(and other pesto purposes)

1 cup water
1½ cups raw unsalted cashews
1 cup fresh basil leaves
1 Tbs. olive oil
1 tsp. Italian seasonings
2 Tbs. soy sauce

Wash the basil. Blenderize all ingredients until smooth. Serve over your favorite pasta. This pesto also makes a good sandwich spread.

Sesame Sandwich Spread
Makes ½ cup

¼ cup tahini
¼ cup water
2 Tbs. nutritional yeast
½ tsp. soy sauce
½ tsp. cumin
¼ tsp. celery salt
¼ tsp. ground mustard

Mix tahini and water in a small bowl. Stir well until combined completely. Mix in yeast, then soy sauce.

Add remaining ingredients and mix well.

Tomato Basil Dressing
Makes 1 cup

1 cup tomato sauce (canned/bottled)
2 tsp. flaxseed oil or olive oil (optional)
1 tsp. lemon juice
20 large fresh basil leaves

Wash basil. Blenderize all ingredients. Serve with your favorite salad.

Quick 'n' Hearty Broccoli,
with romaine lettuce, cherry tomatoes,
pumpernickel bread, and butternut squash

Veggie
Dishes

(Clockwise from top): Robust Yams, Saucy Veggies with Hummus Sauce, spaghetti squash

Candied Yams
Makes one 9" round dish

4 large yams
3 cups water
2½ cups crushed pineapple
½ cup granulated cane juice,
    or brown sugar
2 Tbs. corn starch
½ cup pecans
½ cup maple syrup
1 tsp. cinnamon

Wash, chop, and cook yams in water. Drain, allow to cool, and peel yams. Mix them with the pineapple, sweetener, and corn starch. Put in baking dish.

Chop pecans, and mix in the maple syrup and cinnamon. Pour pecan mix on top of yams.

Bake at 375° F. for 15 to 20 minutes.

"Cheesy" Veggies
Makes 2 servings

¼ head cabbage
1 small head broccoli
    or 1 zucchini squash
¾ cup water
1½ cups butter beans, canned;
    or cooked limas
½ cup Hummus Sauce (see recipe)

Wash and chop cabbage and broccoli; cook in the water. Mix in beans. Drain, reserving broth for drinking.

Serve topped with Hummus Sauce (see recipe).
Great for those who want cheese alternatives.

Good Veggie Combo
Makes 2 servings

1 celery stalk
1 small yellow squash
1 tomato
6 button mushrooms
1 small carrot
½ cup water

Wash, chop, and cook vegetables in water.

Serve as is for a colorful side dish, or topped with Hummus Sauce (see recipe), for a "cheesy" vegetable entrée.

Green Veggies du Jour
Serves 4

½ head broccoli
¼ head cabbage
1 small bunch kale
1 zucchini
water

Wash and chop the vegetables (any other green vegetables can be substituted); put in pot with sufficient cooking water.

Bring to boil, then cook on low until tender.

Greens 'n' Beans
Makes 3 servings

1 cup spinach, fresh or frozen
1½ cups black beans, canned
¾ cup tomato sauce
¼ cup water
10 leaves fresh basil
10 leaves fresh oregano

If using fresh spinach, wash and chop it. Put spinach and water in pot and bring to a boil.

Wash and chop herbs. Mix all ingredients in pot, and serve.

Quick 'n' Hearty Broccoli
Makes 3 servings

1 bunch broccoli
½ lb. mushrooms
1 16-oz. can vegetarian baked beans
1 cup water

Wash and chop broccoli and mushrooms. Put in pot with the water and bring to a boil.

Turn off heat, let sit one minute. Drain (save cooking water to drink as a cup of broth).

Mix the beans in, and serve in individual bowls (or oversized moose-motif mugs). The whole-wheat crackers are optional.

Robust Yams
Makes 4 servings

2 large yams
1 cup dates
1 cup cranberries
1/3 cup shelled walnuts

Peel, wash, and chop yams. Wash cranberries. Pit and chop dates. Mix yams, berries, and dates. Place in loaf pan. Chop walnuts, sprinkle on top.

Cover pan with aluminum foil. Bake at 350° F. for 1 hour 20 minutes, or until yams are tender.

Serve as a colorful side dish.

Smashed Potatoes
Serves 4

6 medium potatoes
water
1 Tbs. nutritional yeast
2 Tbs. diced fresh dill
¾ cup soy milk

Scrub and chop potatoes (not necessary to peel). Cook them in water (bring to boil on high, then simmer until tender).

Drain water, reserving for drinking; or can use some in place of soy milk. Smash potatoes and mash well, using masher, fork, or back of large spoon. Add yeast, dill, and soy milk; mix well.

Serve while still warm. Can be topped with Basic Mushroom Gravy (see recipe).

Succotash Supreme

Makes 4 servings

7 scallions / green onions
1 red bell pepper
1 cup water
1 lb. lima beans, fresh or frozen
1 lb. corn kernels, fresh or frozen

Wash and dice scallions and pepper. Put all ingredients in a pot. Bring to a boil and reduce the heat. Cook for 5 to 10 minutes.

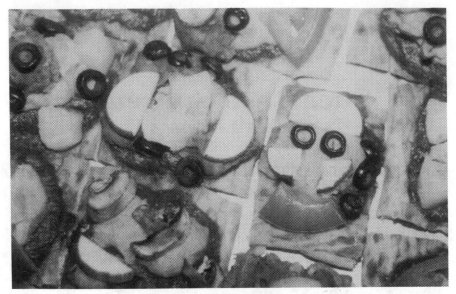

Big Easy Pizza

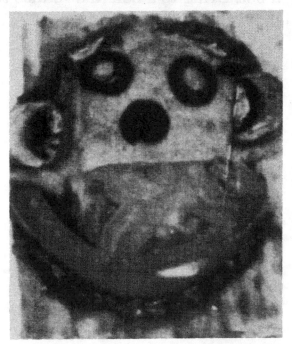

Entrées
and
Casseroles

Cous-Cous Curry-osity

Mushroom Burgers with sandwich fixings
Mushroom Burger sandwich, with
corn on the cob, sliced bell pepper

Triple-Topped Potatoes

Big Easy Pizza
Feeds 4

1 Afghan bread (about 9x24")
1 8-oz. can spaghetti sauce
   or tomato sauce
10 mushrooms
1 green bell pepper
1 large tomato
10 pitted black olives
1 cup meatless soy sausage

(For pre-cut pizza: first cut bread into 3" squares. Reassemble Afghan bread on cookie sheet, with the pieces all touching tightly.)

Spread sauce on the bread.

Wash, pat dry, and chop mushrooms, pepper, tomato, olives. Scatter these and soy sausage over the sauce.

Bake @ 350° F. for 15 minutes.

Black Bean Extravaganza
Makes 5 servings

½ lb. tofu (firm)
1 Tbs. soy sauce
1 Tbs. nutritional yeast (optional)
3 celery stalks
2 carrots
2 cups water
4 plum tomatoes (fresh or canned)
1½ cups black beans (canned, drained)
1 cup tomato sauce

Cut tofu into ¼" cubes. Place on paper towel and pat dry; then put tofu in bowl. Pour soy sauce over tofu and turn gently to coat cubes. Spread one layer thick in small baking pan. Sprinkle with nutritional yeast, and bake at 400° F. for 30 minutes.

Meanwhile, wash, finely chop, and steam (or cook) celery and carrots. Drain (always save broth for drinking or use as stock), and mix in baked tofu and all other ingredients.

Serve with Corn Bread Muffins (see recipe).

Brussels Sprout Surprise
Makes 4 to 6 servings

1 bunch broccoli
¼ head cabbage
2 cups water
3 cups frozen cut corn, thawed
1/8 cup additional water
(or save from cooking)
1 tsp. celery salt
2 tsp. cumin
1 Tbs. oil
2 celery stalks

Wash and chop the broccoli and cabbage. Cook them in the 2 cups water, then drain. Some cooking water can be saved to re-use as the 1/8 cup water.

Blend corn, celery salt, cumin, oil, celery, and 1/8 cup water, to make a corn sauce.

Put drained vegetables in loaf pan. Mix in some of the sauce. Pour the rest of the sauce on top to cover vegetables.

Bake @ 350° F. for 20 to 30 minutes.

The surprise is that there are no Brussels sprouts under the sauce. For variation, use Brussels sprouts instead of broccoli, and call it Broccoli Surprise.

Celery-Mushroom Stuffing
Makes 1 loaf (6 servings)

3 celery stalks
20 whole button mushrooms
¼ cup fresh cilantro
4 cups whole wheat bread
    (4 large slices: crust or dry is good)
1 Tbs. sage
1 tsp. celery salt
1 tsp. Italian seasoning
½ tsp. paprika
2 cups vegetable broth
1 tsp. corn starch

Wash and chop celery, mushrooms and cilantro. Cut bread into small cubes. Mix all ingredients. Lightly pack into loaf pan, and bake at 350° F. for 45 minutes.

Serve with Basic Mushroom Gravy (see recipe). Good with Smashed Potatoes (see recipe) and steamed broccoli.

Cous-Cous Curry-osity
Makes 6 servings

2 large white potatoes
1 small butternut squash
1½ cups water
2 Tbs. soy sauce, tamari
2 Tbs. corn starch
2 tsp. curry powder
½ cup raisins
1 15-oz. can chick peas (garbanzos)

1½ cups cous-cous
3 cups water

VEGGIES: Peel squash. Wash and chop potatoes and squash. Put in pot with 1½ cups water. Bring to boil; reduce heat and cook until potatoes are tender.

Meanwhile, in separate container, mix soy sauce, corn starch and curry powder until smooth. Then mix it into the hot water in which the squash and potatoes are still cooking.

Remove from heat. Stir in raisins & chick peas.

COUS-COUS: Put cous-cous and 3 cups water in a pot. Bring to boil. Remove from heat and let stand 10 minutes. Fluff with a fork.

Serve the veggies on top of the cous-cous.

Eat Your Veggies Spaghetti
Serves 4

½ lb. whole wheat spaghetti
10 cups water
2 small yellow summer squash
2 small zucchini squash
3 celery stalks
1 green bell pepper
2 tomatoes
Dash of Italian herbs
2 cups tomato sauce
1 Tbs. olive oil

Bring water to a boil in a large pot. Add pasta, stirring gently until it boils again. Cook for 5 to 10 minutes, until tender. Drain and remove from pot.

Meanwhile, wash and chop vegetables. In the empty pot, put the oil, vegetables, and herbs. Stir constantly over medium-high heat for 5 to 10 minutes, until veggies are tender, yet still fresh and not mushy. Add the tomato sauce and spaghetti. Mix and serve.

Green Bean Casserole

4 cups green beans
2 cups water
3 cups Mushroom Soup
(made now or day before; see recipe)
1/8 cup wheat germ,
whole wheat bread crumbs,
or corn chips, crushed
extra bread crumbs if needed

Wash and chop green beans (diagonal slices are a nice touch). Put in pot with water; cook until tender but not mushy. Drain off cooking water (you can drink this or save for making a gravy later).

Mix beans with soup (the soup should be thick, not runny; mix in extra bread crumbs if needed to thicken). Place in small casserole pan. Sprinkle wheat germ on top. Bake at 350° F. for 20 to 30 minutes (a few minutes less if soup is already hot).

Macaroni Casserole
Makes 12 servings

8 cups water
½ head red or green cabbage
1 large head broccoli
3 cups whole wheat macaroni
3 cups tomato juice
1 cup raw unsalted cashew nuts
1 tsp. celery salt
2 Tbs. nutritional yeast

Boil water in a large pot.

Wash and chop cabbage and broccoli. Add these and the macaroni to boiling water, and stir. Bring to a boil again and reduce heat. Cook for 5 to 10 minutes or until macaroni is tender but not mushy.

Meanwhile, place the remaining ingredients in blender. Blend to make a smooth sauce. Drain vegetables and pasta, and place in casserole pan. Pour in sauce and stir.

Bake at 375° F. for 15 minutes.

Mushroom Burgers
Makes 2

2 Portabella mushrooms
   (about 4" caps; or 8 baby Portabellas)
1 Tbs. olive oil
2 Tbs. soy sauce
Dash of pepper
Dash of ginger
6 leaves of fresh chopped basil (optional)
   or dash of dried basil

Wash and pat dry mushrooms. Separate stems from caps. Place oil and soy sauce in pan. Turn on medium heat. Add mushroom caps and stir, flipping occasionally.

When caps begin to water, add stems and seasonings. Continue cooking and stirring for 2 to 3 minutes. The water will begin to dry as the pleasant aroma becomes noticeable.

Serve on a whole wheat bun or sliced bread, with lettuce, tomato and ketchup, or with your favorite fixings.

Mushroom Stroganoff
Makes 4 servings

Mushroom sauce:
   1 cup (½ lb.) mushrooms
   1/3 cup dulse
   1 cup water
   1 cup soy milk
   2 Tbs. corn starch
   1/8 tsp. cayenne pepper (optional)

Pasta:
   ½ lb. whole wheat fettucini pasta
   2 quarts water

Garnish:
   ¼ cup fresh parsley

Wash and chop mushrooms. Gently wash dulse.

Mix in pot: 1 cup water, soy milk, corn starch, and pepper. Add dulse and mushrooms.

Bring to a rapid boil, stirring constantly while it begins to thicken. Remove from heat; it will thicken more as it cools.

In a separate pot, bring 2 quarts of water to a boil. Stir in pasta and return to rapid boil, stirring frequently. Reduce heat and cook for 10 minutes.

Drain pasta. Serve with mushroom sauce poured over. Wash and finely chop the parsley, to use as garnish on top.

Pizza Cheese
Makes 3 to 4 cups

1½ cups nutritional yeast flakes
½ cup whole wheat pastry flour
1/3 cup corn starch
3 cups water
2 Tbs. oil
1 tsp. salt

Mix yeast, flour, and corn starch. While stirring, add water gradually to prevent lumps.

Heat in pot on stove. Stir constantly, scraping bottom, until it all thickens.

Remove from heat. Stir in oil and salt.

This recipe is used on pizza, vegan lasagna, or other items that will be further baked.

Portabella Polenta
Makes 6 servings

3½ cups water
1 cup corn meal
2 zucchini squash
2 tomatoes
4 small portabella mushrooms
½ tsp. Italian seasoning herbs

First make the polenta: Boil 2 cups of the water. Mix 1 cup of the cold water with corn meal, and mix into the boiling water. Reduce heat and cook for 30 minutes. Stir frequently to prevent sticking.

Meanwhile, wash and chop vegetables. In a separate pot, cook the veggies, with ½ cup water and seasonings, for 5 to 10 minutes.

Serve vegetables over the corn meal polenta.

Quick Pizza Slices
Makes 4 slices

4 slices whole wheat bread
½ cup spaghetti sauce
1½ cups black beans (canned, drained)
1 cup Pizza Cheese (see recipe)
8 green olives

Place bread on baking sheet. Spread spaghetti sauce on bread. Slice olives.

Place beans, Pizza Cheese, and olives on sauce.

Bake at 350° F. for 15 minutes, or until cheese begins to turn golden brown.

Roasted Veggies
Serves 6

4 small potatoes
2 celery stalks
10 Brussels sprouts
2 carrots
1 Tbs. olive oil
2 tsp. soy sauce
1 tsp. cumin
½ tsp. paprika
¼ tsp. chili powder
¼ tsp. coriander
1 Tbs. nutritional yeast
1 tsp. corn starch

Wash and chop veggies. Mix veggies, oil, and soy sauce. Mix all remaining ingredients and sprinkle on the veggies. Gently stir. Place in non-stick or lightly-oiled casserole pan, and cover with aluminum foil.

Bake @ 375° F. for 20 to 30 minutes, or until veggies are tender. For a crispier taste, remove foil, stir and bake an additional 5 to 10 minutes.

Spinach Lasagna
Makes 12 servings

1 lb. spinach (fresh or frozen)
1 lb. or 1 large head broccoli
8 cups water
½ lb. whole wheat lasagna
3 cups spaghetti sauce
3 cups Pizza Cheese (see recipe)

If spinach and broccoli are fresh, wash and chop. If frozen, just open bag. Boil water in large pot. Add lasagna and veggies.

The pasta must be loosely arranged, submerged, but not stuck together. Lightly stir to prevent sticking to sides or bottom of pan. (Add more boiling water if necessary.) Lower heat, cook until pasta is tender. Drain through strainer or colander.

In a large oiled or non-stick casserole pan, layer half of each: veggies, pasta, sauce, and "cheese." Repeat layers, finishing with "cheese" on top.

Bake at 350° F. for 30 minutes, or until done.

Note: Also good with other vegetables, such as cabbage, squash, etc.; or you can add a layer of vegan "sausage" (meat substitute).

Stuffed Mushrooms
Makes 6 servings

6 large stuffable mushrooms
¼ cup brown rice, cooked in
    ½ cup water for 40 minutes
    (or 1 cup cooked rice)
½ cup vegan "sausage," crumbled
1 small carrot
¼ red bell pepper
½ cup spaghetti sauce

Wash mushrooms. Remove and save the stems. Place caps upside-down on baking pan.

Wash and grate carrot. Wash and finely chop pepper.

Make stuffing by mixing all ingredients except mushroom caps and stems. Generously fill each cap with stuffing, gently patting into a mound. Place a stem on top of each stuffing mound.

Bake at 350° F. for 15 minutes.

Super Potato Pie
Makes 6 servings

4 medium potatoes
1½ cups water
1 large leek
2 celery stalks
2 carrots
1 tomato
1 cup water
1½ cups garbanzos (cooked or canned)
1 cup tomato sauce
1 tsp. Italian seasonings herbs

Wash and chop potatoes; cook in 1½ cups water. Partially drain (save the water), and mash.

Add cooking water gradually to make a thick creamy consistency, not runny or dry.

While potatoes are cooking, prepare vegetables. Wash and finely chop leek, celery, carrots, and tomato. Cook the vegetables in 1 cup water, and drain (saving water for drinks, broth, or to mix in potatoes). Mix in garbanzos, tomato sauce, and herbs.

Put veggie mixture into pie pan and top with mashed potatoes. Can be served as is, or bake at 350° F. for 10 to 15 minutes.

Tempting Tempeh
Serves 2

1 8-oz. block tempeh
1/8 cup soy sauce

Cut tempeh into 2-inch squares. Dip them in soy sauce. Place in baking dish.

Bake @ 350° F. for about 10 minutes, or until edges are slightly crispy brown.

Great served warm as an entrée, or can be put in a sandwich as a "burger."

Triple-Topped Potatoes
Serves 4

1 small head broccoli
¼ cup water
4 large potatoes
1 cup Pizza Cheese (see recipe)
1 cup baked beans (canned, vegetarian)

Wash potatoes. Bake them at 375° F. for 1 hour or until tender.

Meanwhile, wash and chop broccoli, and place in microwaveable bowl with water. Microwave on high for 3 minutes or until slightly tender but still bright green.

Slice open baked potatoes and place in baking pan. Smother potatoes with broccoli, beans, and cheese.

Bake at 350° F. for 10 minutes or until cheese begins to turn golden brown.

Veggeroni

Makes 6 servings

6 cups water
1½ cups whole wheat macaroni
1 lb. bag frozen mixed vegetables
3½ cups whole tomatoes (can), or
**   fresh tomatoes, chopped**
10 leaves fresh basil

Bring the water to a boil. Add macaroni and vegetables, and bring to a boil again. Cook on low for 8 to 10 minutes.

Wash and chop basil. Drain the macaroni and vegetables. Add tomatoes and basil. Mix and serve.

Breads and Muffins

Banana Muffins and Bread
Makes 12 muffins and 1 loaf bread

5 bananas
¾ cup molasses
¼ cup oil
1 cup orange juice
1 cup pecans
1 cup raisins

3 cups whole wheat pastry flour
2 Tbs. cornstarch
1 Tbs. baking soda
1 Tbs. pumpkin pie spices

11/3 cups whole wheat bread flour

Whisk together the molasses, oil, and orange juice. Mash and stir in bananas. Chop pecans; mix with all other dry ingredients except whole wheat bread flour.

Combine the mixtures and stir. Use half of the batter in lightly oiled or non-stick muffin tins. Add the bread flour to the rest of the batter, and pour into lightly oiled or non-stick loaf pan.

Bake @ 375° F., muffins about 15 minutes and bread about 20 minutes, or until done.

Cornbread Muffins
Makes 12 muffins

¾ cup soy milk
½ Tbs. oil
2 Tbs. molasses
½ Tbs. baking soda
1/3 cup oats
1/3 cup whole wheat pastry flour
1½ cups corn meal

Mix wet ingredients and dry ingredients separately. Combine them and stir. Put in lightly oiled or non-stick muffin tins, and bake at 350° F. for 35 minutes.

Good topped with jelly for breakfast; or serve with Black Bean Extravaganza (see recipe) for dinner.

Gingerbread
Makes 16 squares

½ cups dates, pitted
½ cup raisins
1¼ cups water
¾ cup granulated cane juice,
   or brown sugar
1 Tbs. pumpkin pie spices
2 cups whole wheat pastry flour
2 tsp. baking soda
2 tsp. cornstarch

Blenderize dates, raisins, and water. Mix all other ingredients separately, then stir in date mixture. Pour into two lightly oiled or non-stick loaf pans about an inch deep. Bake @ 350° F. for 20 minutes. Allow to cool and then cut into squares.

Serve with applesauce and/or your favorite non-dairy ice cream.

Pumpkin Muffins

3½ cups pumpkin (1 can)
¼ cup oil
½ cup molasses
½ cup raisins
1 banana, mashed

1½ Tbs. pumpkin pie spices
1½ cups whole wheat pastry flour
1 Tbs. cornstarch
1 tsp. baking soda

Mix wet ingredients. Mix dry ingredients separately. Combine the two mixtures and stir.

Pour the batter into lightly oiled or non-stick muffin tins. Push the raisins under the surface, completely covered so they don't burn.

Bake @ 350° F. for 30 minutes.

Zucchini Bread
Makes 2 loaves

1 extra-large (or 2 medium) zucchini
2 apples
1 banana
1 cup dates, pitted
1 cup walnuts, shelled
1/3 cup molasses

¼ tsp. allspice
½ tsp. cinnamon
2 cups quick oats
1 Tbs. baking soda
3½ cups whole wheat pastry flour
2 Tbs. corn starch

Wash and grate the zucchinis. Wash, core and grate apples. Mash banana. Chop the dates and walnuts. Mix these five items together with the molasses. Mix all remaining ingredients. Combine the two mixes and stir.

Put into two oiled and lightly floured loaf pans; bake at 350° F. for one hour.

Tastes best if allowed to cool at room temperature for a day before eating or refrigerating.

Serve topped with jelly.

Beverages

Cashew Milk
Makes 2¼ cups

¼ cup cashew nuts, raw unsalted
2 cups water
5 dates, pitted
1 Tbs. soy powder (optional)

Blenderize all ingredients until smooth.
Good as a drink, on cereal, in desserts, or in smoothies.

Cashew Smoothie
Makes about 2 cups

1 cup Cashew Milk (see recipe)
2 bananas, peeled and frozen

Blenderize. Serve in 1 extra large or 2 medium glasses.

Festive Mango Punch
Makes 1 glassful

1 cup apple/mango juice
1 cup water
juice of ½ lemon
3 ice cubes
3 mint leaves

Mix liquids in glass. Add ice cubes and mint.

Limeade
Makes 1 large glass

1 lime
1½ cups water
2 Tbs. dried cane juice, or brown sugar

Squeeze the lime to make juice.
Add water and sweetener.
Mix and drink.

New Lemonade
Makes about a pint

1 cup water
1 cup apple juice
1½ Tbs. lemon juice

Mix and drink.

Old Fashioned Lemonade
Makes nearly a pint

1½ cups water
1½ Tbs. lemon juice
2 Tbs. maple syrup

Mix and drink.

Strawberry Shake
Makes 2 servings

1 cup strawberries
½ cup soy milk
   or Cashew Milk (see recipe)
3 bananas, peeled and frozen

Wash and hull berries. Blenderize ingredients.

Desserts

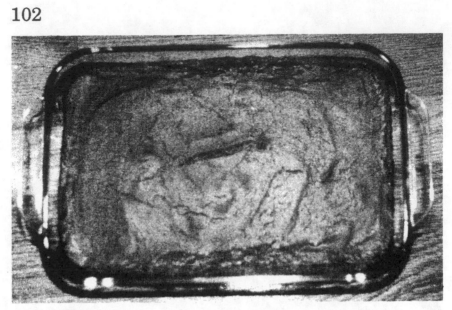

Pumpkin Pie

....with Tofu Whipped Topping

Apple Cobbler
Makes 6 servings

3 apples
12 dates (optional)
1 Tbs. corn starch
½ tsp. cinnamon
1 cup maple syrup
1 cup whole wheat pastry flour

Wash and chop apples. Pit and chop dates. Mix apples, dates, corn starch, and cinnamon. Put in loaf pan.

Mix maple syrup and flour, and pour over the apples.

Bake at 375° F. for 30 to 40 minutes, or until done. Serve with Tofu Whipped Topping or Coconut Cream (see the recipes). This recipe also works well with other fruits instead of apples; or replace 1 apple with rhubarb.

Carrot Cake
Makes 12 servings

1 cup soy milk
4 carrots
2 bananas
2 Tbs. oil
½ cup molasses

1 tsp. pumpkin pie spices
2 tsp. baking soda
2½ cups whole wheat pastry flour

1 cup shelled walnuts
1 cup dates

Wash and chop carrots. Peel bananas. Place in blender: soy milk, carrots, bananas, oil, molasses. Blenderize until smooth.

Mix spices, soda, and flour.

Pit the dates, chop the dates and walnuts. Stir them into the dry flour mix. Then add the blenderized mixture and stir together.

Place in large cake or casserole pan. Bake at 375° F. for 40 minutes, or until done.

Chocomint Pudding
Makes 4 servings

½ cup water
1 peppermint tea bag
2 cups soy milk
¼ cup unsweetened cocoa powder
2 Tbs. corn starch
1/3 cup granulated cane juice,
   or brown sugar

Boil water. Place tea bag in hot water for three minutes. Remove bag. Pour this strong tea into blender.

Add remaining ingredients and blenderize.

Pour into pot. Stir while bringing to boil on medium heat, scraping the bottom constantly until mixture thickens.

Remove from heat. Chill and serve.

Chocorange Cupcakes
Makes 12

1 cup orange juice
½ lb. tofu (firm)
1 cup granulated cane juice
   or other sweetener
1/3 cup unsweetened carob
   (or cocoa) powder
1 Tbs. baking soda
2 tsp. orange peel
½ tsp. ginger
11/3 cups whole wheat pastry flour
   or unbleached flour

Blenderize all ingredients except the flour, and pour into bowl. Mix in flour.

Put into non-stick or lightly oiled muffin tins. Bake at 350° F. for 20 minutes. Let cool.

Serve cupcakes topped with Chocorange Icing (see recipe).

Chocorange Icing

Covers 1 cake or tops 18 cupcakes

1 cup orange juice
2/3 cup unsweetened
 carob (or cocoa) powder
1 cup granulated cane juice
 or other sweetener
1/3 cup corn starch
½ tsp. ginger

Blenderize all ingredients. Pour into pot. Heat on medium-high. Stir constantly, scraping bottom until the mix thickens.

Use for cake icing (such as Chocorange Cupcakes—see recipe), or as a finger-lickin' dessert by itself.

Coconut Cream
Makes 1 1/3 cups

1 Tbs. shredded coconut
½ lb. tofu
¼ cup maple syrup
2 Tbs. lemon juice
3 Tbs. soy milk

Blenderize. Serve over desserts such as cakes or cobblers. (See Tomato Soup Cake, Apple Cobbler.)

Cranberry Cake
Makes 2 loaves

1 lime
1¼ cups maple syrup
½ lb. tofu (firm)
2 Tbs. corn starch
1 Tbs. baking soda
2 cups whole wheat pastry flour
½ tsp. ground cinnamon
½ tsp. ground cloves
2 bananas
3 cups cranberries
1 cup dates
2/3 cup shelled walnuts or pecans
2/3 cup carob chips or chocolate chips

Juice the lime. Blenderize lime juice, maple syrup, and tofu. In a large bowl mix the corn starch, soda, flour, and spices. Then mix in the blenderized liquid.

Mash bananas. Wash cranberries. Chop dates and nuts. Mix all ingredients. Place in two non-stick or lightly-oiled loaf pans. Bake at 375° F. for 30 minutes, or until done.

Serve sliced, either warm or cool.

Cran-Wheat Treat
Serves 4

¼ cup tahini
¼ cup molasses
1¼ cups puffed wheat
1 cup Cranberry Sauce (see recipe)

Mix tahini and molasses. Add puffed wheat and mix well (without smashing cereal).

Swirl in cranberry sauce.

Place in 4 bowls. Chill in freezer. Serve.

Currant Carrot Cookies
Makes 32 cookies

3 carrots
¼ cup oil
½ cup rice syrup or other sweetener
½ cup orange juice

1½ cups quick oats
1¼ cups whole wheat pastry flour
1 tsp. baking soda
½ tsp. ginger
¾ cup currants

Wash and shred carrots, then mix with wet ingredients. In separate bowl, mix all remaining ingredients. Combine wet and dry mixes, and stir.

Drop by heaping tablespoonfuls onto a non-stick or lightly oiled cooky sheet.

Bake 20 minutes at 350° F. or until golden brown.

Currant Clusters
Makes 20

1 banana, mashed
½ cup applesauce
1 cup currants
2 Tbs. soy milk
¾ cup granulated cane juice
  or other sweetener
¼ tsp. salt
½ cup pecans
3 cups puffed wheat
½ cup shredded coconut (optional)

Place in a pot: mashed banana, applesauce, currants, soy milk, sweetener, and salt. Boil for two minutes, stirring occasionally.

Chop pecans. Mix pecans and puffed wheat into the pot.

Drop onto plate by heaping tablespoons. Each cluster can be rolled in shredded coconut.

Gooball

Makes oodles (12 large handfuls)

3 bananas
2 apples
½ cup applesauce
1 cup molasses
¼ cup water
¾ cup apple juice

1 Tbs. baking soda
½ cup raisins
2 cups oats
2½ cups whole wheat pastry flour
¾ tsp. ginger
¼ tsp. cloves

Peel and mash bananas. Wash and chop the apples. Mix first six (wet mix) ingredients and last six (dry mix) ingredients in two separate bowls. Combine them and stir. You can also add small amounts of optional "secret" ingredients that your friends won't guess: dates, filberts, nutmeg, wheat germ, cinnamon, figs, a strawberry or blueberry, etc.

Put in casserole pan. Bake at 350° F. about 40 minutes. The middle should be moist, not wet. Let cool. Take handfuls to make into shapes and eat; fun for playful guests to do (if too dry to mold, add a bit of extra juice). Tastes especially good accompanied by vegan "ice cream."

Mango Cream Pie
(Easy) - Serves 2

1 ripe mango
2 cups Tofu Banana Freeze (see recipe)
¼ cup carob chips

Peel and pit mango. Line 2 individual bowls with mango pieces: mango is the "crust" of the pie. Pour in the Tofu Banana Freeze. Sprinkle top with carob chips.

Serve and eat before it melts.

Pear Cobbler #1
Makes 12 servings

6 pears
¼ cup molasses
½ cup raisins
2 Tbs. cornstarch
¼ cup wheat germ, toasted
¼ cup shredded coconut
½ cup quick oats
2 tsp. oil
1 tsp. cinnamon

Wash, core, and chop pears. Add and mix in the molasses, raisins, and cornstarch.

In a separate bowl, make topping by mixing wheat germ, coconut, and oats. Add the oil, and stir in before it gets absorbed.

Put pear mixture in casserole dish. Spread topping on pear mixture. Sprinkle cinnamon on top. Bake @ 350° F. for 10 to 15 minutes, until top begins to brown; pears are warmed, not cooked.

Pear Cobbler #2
Makes 12 servings

6 pears
¼ cup maple syrup
½ cup dates
2 Tbs. cornstarch
2/3 cup whole wheat pastry flour
1 tsp. baking soda
¼ cup shredded coconut
1 tsp. cinnamon
½ cup soy milk

Wash, core, and chop pears. Pit and chop dates. Mix pears, dates, maple syrup, and cornstarch.

In a separate bowl, make topping by mixing flour, soda, coconut, and cinnamon. Add the soy milk and stir it in.

Put pear mixture in casserole dish. Spread topping on pear mixture.

Bake @ 350° F. for 20 to 30 minutes, until top begins to brown.

Puffed Treats
Makes 8

¼ cup tahini
¼ cup molasses
1¼ cups puffed wheat or puffed rice

Mix tahini and molasses. Add the puffed cereal, and stir well.

Drop by large spoonfuls onto a plate. Chill in freezer. Serve.

Pumpkin Pie
Makes two 9"-diameter pies

1 29-oz. can pumpkin
1 cup maple syrup
½ cup soy milk
½ lb. tofu
1 tsp. cinnamon
1 tsp. ginger
½ cup apple juice
4 cups corn flakes or 2 cups granola

Mix juice and cereal. Pour into pie pans and level out for "crust."

Put puréed pumpkin into a mixing bowl. Blenderize maple syrup, soy milk, tofu, and spices. Stir into pumpkin to make filling.

Pour filling into pans. Bake at 350° F. for 30 minutes or until done. Cool.

Serve with Tofu Whipped Topping or Coconut Cream (see recipes).

Rice Pudding
Makes 10-12 servings

¾ cup brown rice
1½ cups water
½ cup molasses
1½ cups soy milk
2 cups crushed pineapple (canned)
½ tsp. ginger
2 Tbs. tahini
1 cup raisins
additional soy milk (optional)

Wash rice, put it in a pot with the water. Bring to boil, then turn down and simmer about 45 minutes, or until the rice is cooked and water absorbed.

Stir in remaining ingredients. Put the mix in two loaf pans or a casserole dish. Bake @ 350° F. for one hour.

Serve warm or cold, in bowls. Pour additional soy milk around pudding, if desired.

Rich Almond Pudding
Makes 2 servings

¼ cup raw almonds (shelled)
1 cup dates
2½ cups water

Put almonds in 2 cups of the water and bring to a boil on stove or in microwave. Allow to cool. Blanch almonds (remove their skins).

Pit the dates. Place almonds, dates, and ½ cup water in blender. Blenderize until smooth, and serve.

Sticky Little Worlds
Makes 10

1 cup dates, pitted
½ cup soy milk
1 Tbs. corn starch
¼ tsp. pumpkin pie spices
2 Tbs. tahini
1/8 cup shredded coconut

Blenderize all ingredients except coconut. Put in microwave bowl. Cover with plate. Zap on high for three minutes. Stir and allow to cool. It will continue to thicken.

Form into ten one-inch diameter globes. Sprinkle with coconut.

Alternative method of preparation (this method may be lumpier): Boil dates and soy milk. Mash, then mix in starch, spices, and tahini. Stir while re-boiling, until it thickens. Cool. Form globes as above.

Strawberry Shortcake
Makes 8 servings

2 cups whole wheat pastry flour
1 Tbs. baking soda
1 Tbs. corn starch

2 Tbs. maple syrup
1 cup applesauce
1 cup soy milk

1 quart strawberries
1 cup additional maple syrup

Mix first three ingredients (dry). In separate bowl, mix next three items (wet), then combine with the dry mixture, and stir. Pour into large casserole pan, and bake at 350° F. for 20 to 25 minutes. Allow to cool.

Meanwhile, wash and drain the strawberries. Hull them and cut them in half. Mix in 1 cup of maple syrup.

Carefully cut cake in half horizontally (to make two thin layers). Place one layer on serving platter. Pour 1 cup of berry mix on it. Put other cake layer on top of the berries on the first layer. Pour remaining berry mix on top. Some will fall to the sides.

Top with Tofu Whipped Topping (see recipe), and serve with a glassful of soy milk.

Tofu Banana Freeze
Makes 2 servings

**½ lb. tofu
2 large bananas, peeled and frozen**

Blenderize tofu and bananas. A banana can be used to push ingredients down while blending, but keep fingers well away from blades. Eat promptly.

Variations: Mix in or add on top, any of these: fresh fruits, nuts, maple syrup, dried fruits, etc.

Tofu Whipped Topping
Makes 11/3 cups

½ lb. tofu (firm)
1/3 cup maple syrup
1 Tbs. lemon juice
¼ tsp. ginger

Blenderize all the ingredients. Serve on pies or other desserts.

Tomato Soup Cake
(A spice cake)
Makes one 9x12" cake

2 cups tomato soup
¾ cup water
¾ cup molasses
¾ cup maple syrup
¼ cup oil
1 Tbs. baking soda
3 cups whole wheat pastry flour
2 tsp. cinnamon
1 tsp. ground cloves
1 cup raisins
1 cup shelled walnuts

Mix all wet ingredients. Chop walnuts. Mix dry ingredients. Combine everything, stir, and put into a casserole pan.

Bake at 350° F. for approximately one hour.

(Nobody ever guesses it has tomato soup in it!)

INDEX

AVS/Ahimsa Publications

The COILED SERPENT

The Vegan Kitchen

Editorial from #30-03 Ahimsa magazine

"Cruelty-

Vegan Be

Gandhian Truth-Force & No
BY H. JAY DINSHAH

Overweight
and

LISTING OF INGREDIENTS AND MATERIALS:
Animal, Vegetable, Mi

H. Jay Dinshah's
OUT OF THE JUNGLE
The Way of Dynamic Harmlessness

MOSTLY ABOUT ALCOHOL
by

Don't Let Them
Pull The Wool
Ove
EASY VEGAN RECIPES

Vegan Organic Gardening A

What Happens
To The
Calf?

Here's Harmlessness

An Anthology
Of Ahimsa

Let's Go Vegan!

HEALTH
Can Be
HARMLESS
H. Jay Dinshah

VEGANISM:
GETTING
STARTED

Ahimsa

Now
Try
VEGANISM!

The Myth About Milk

Simply A Better Life

39TH ANNUAL AVS CONVENTION

COMPASSION
THE ULTIMATE ETHIC
An Exploration of Veganism

Send for free sample copy of Ahimsa magazine:

The American Vegan Society
56 Dinshah Lane — P.O. Box H
Malaga, New Jersey 08328

A Non-Profit Educational Organization
Lighting The Way Since 1960